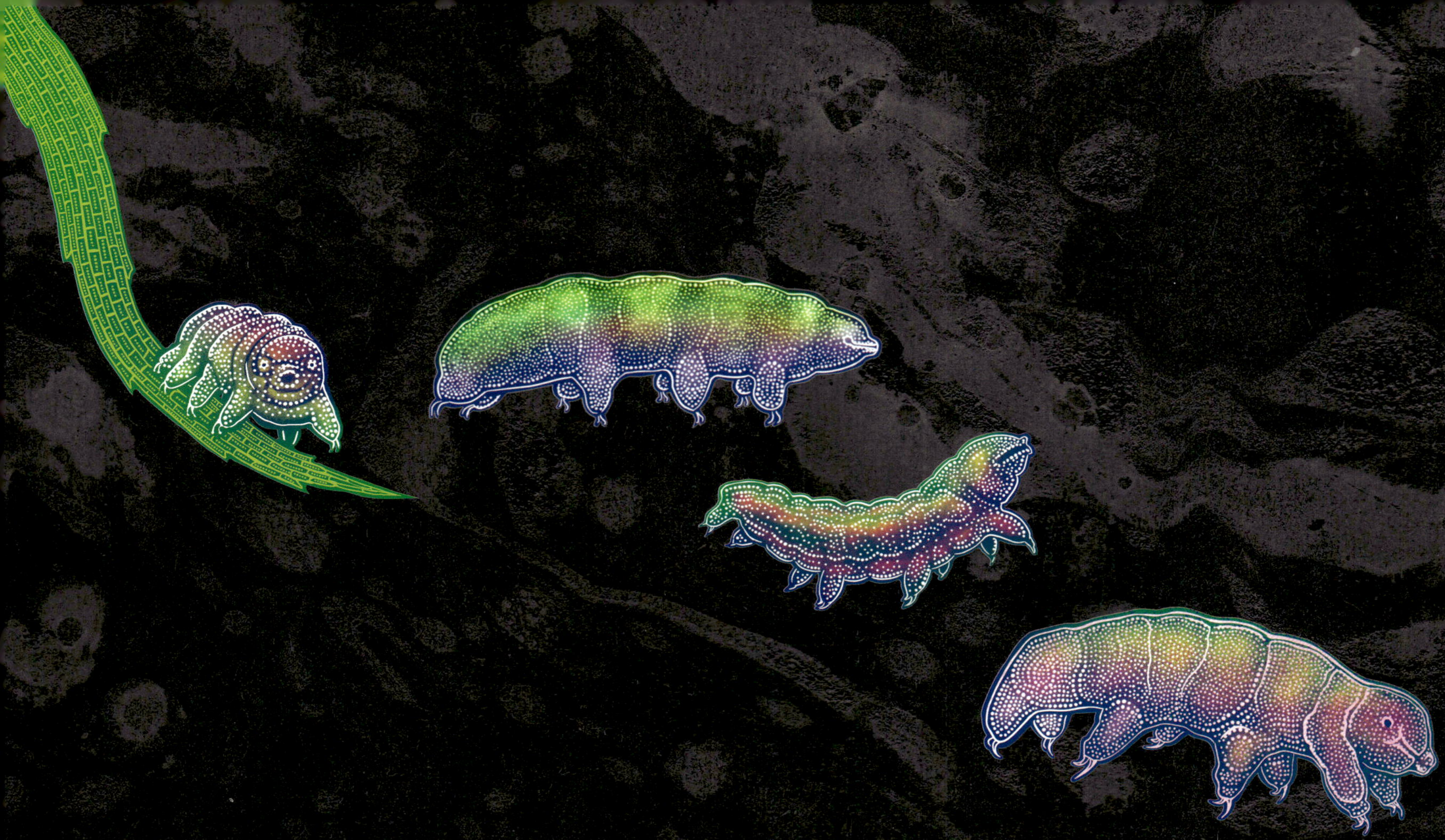

For Benji and Alex, the littlest members of the family. Lots of love, Auntie Jenny. – *J.S.*

First published in the United Kingdom in 2026 by
Thames & Hudson Ltd, 6–24 Britannia Street, London WC1X 9JD

Consultancy by Dr George Janes

EU Authorized Representative: Interart S.A.R.L.
19 rue Charles Auray, 93500 Pantin, Paris, France
productsafety@thameshudson.co.uk
interart.fr

A CIP catalogue record for this book is available from the British Library

ISBN 978-0-500-65403-3
01

Printed in China by RR Donnelley

MIX
Paper | Supporting responsible forestry
FSC® C144853

JENNIFER N. R. SMITH

MICRO

the WILD WONDERS of MICROSCOPIC LIFE

CONTENTS

1.

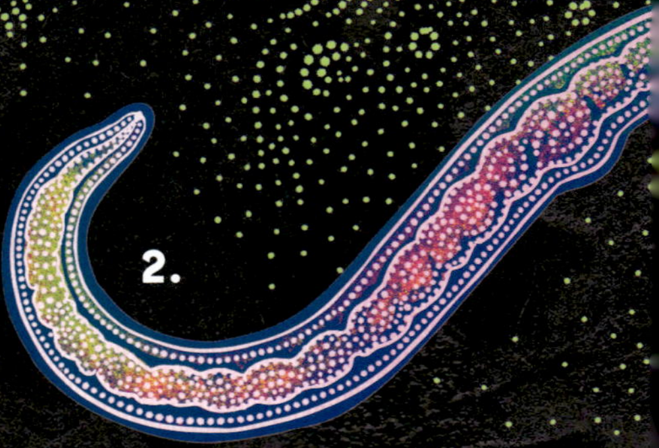

2.

BEYOND OUR EYES

IN A DEEP, DARK FOREST, UNDER AN OLD, GNARLED TREE, there is a small, damp patch of moss. To our eyes, not much is going on in this little clump of fuzzy greenery. But if we were to zoom in beyond what our eyes can see, we would discover a hub of activity – a moss metropolis! A tardigrade – also known as a 'water bear' or 'moss piglet' – waddles by on its 8 squishy legs. A nematode wiggles its wormy body. An amoeba absorbs its prey directly into its jelly-like body.

There is a hidden world all around us, unseen to the naked eye. But how do we know this is going on? It's all thanks to a very clever invention, the microscope.

Microscopes are magnificent tools that magnify objects, allowing us to see fine details or things that would otherwise be too small to see.

MICRO means 'small', and **SCOPE** means 'to look at'.

Under the **lens** of a microscope, the familiar is transformed into a spectacle that can be strange, beautiful and sometimes even a little frightening!

Prepare to go on a sightseeing tour of this hidden microscopic world that surrounds us. In this book, you will travel through different landscapes to discover the tiny terrains within them, meet new creatures and uncover the mini building blocks that are the foundation of our planet.

PLATE KEY

1. TARDIGRADE 2. NEMATODE 3. AMOEBA
4. **GASTROTRICH** 5. CILIATE 6. ROTIFER 7. MOSS MITE

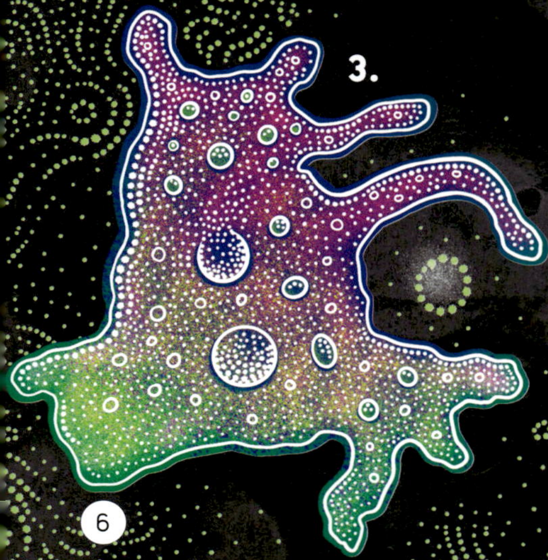

3.

4.

5.
6.
7.

HOW MICROSCOPES WORK

THERE ARE SEVERAL TYPES OF MICROSCOPES.

They work in different ways and have different uses. The samples that are collected and viewed under microscopes are called specimens.

OPTICAL MICROSCOPES

These microscopes use lenses. Lenses are curved, transparent pieces of glass or plastic that bend light as it passes through them. When you look through a lens, objects on the other side of it appear bigger or closer. This is called **magnification**. Optical microscopes can magnify up to around 2,000x – which means they can make things appear 2,000 times larger than their real size.

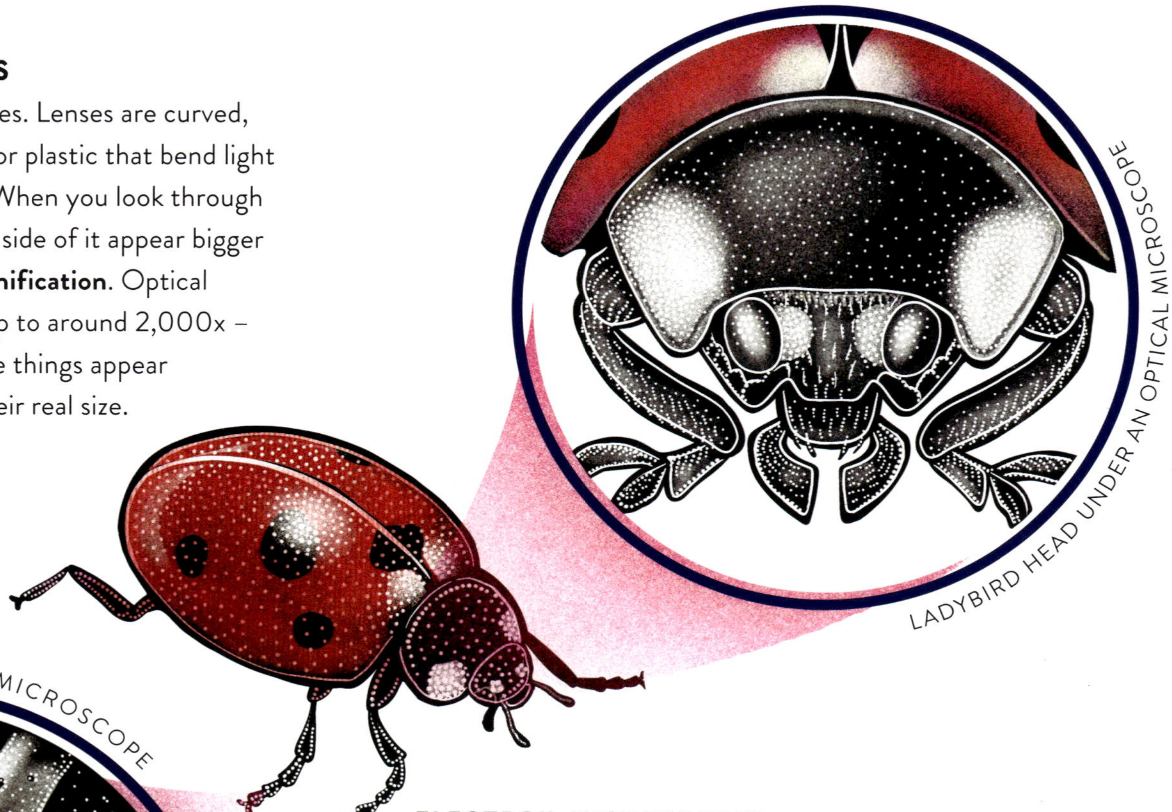

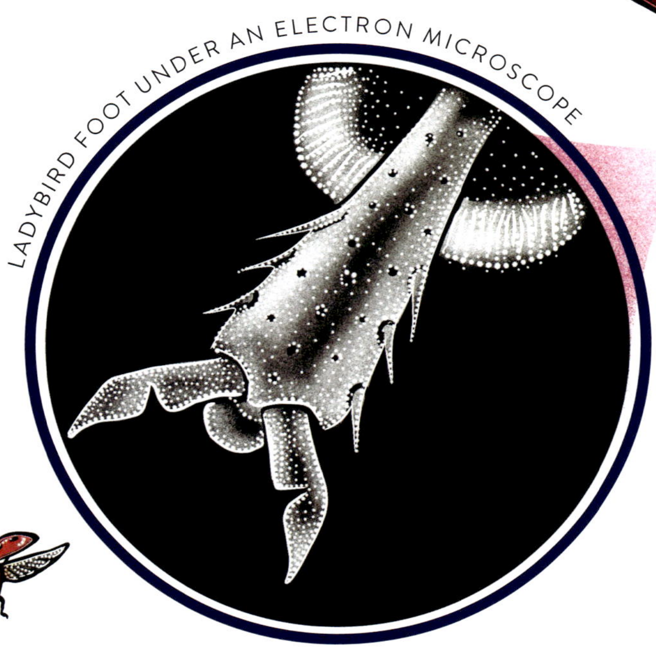

ELECTRON MICROSCOPES

Electron microscopes are much more powerful than optical microscopes and can magnify millions of times more. This is because they use beams of **electrons** instead of light, which can pass through smaller spaces. They create a picture of a specimen, which is viewed on a screen rather than through an eyepiece. For this type of microscope to work, specimens must be coated in a very fine layer of metal, such as gold. This means a drawback to using electron microscopes is that specimens must be dead, and the images show them as opaque and colourless, even when they're not.

HOW TO USE AN OPTICAL MICROSCOPE

The most common microscopes you'll find in schools are optical microscopes. Here's how to use one:

1. Place your microscope on a table and position it so you can look down the eyepiece comfortably.
2. Place your prepared **slide** or **petri dish** containing your specimen over the hole in the stage.
3. Turn on the in-built lamp under the stage to light your specimen.
4. Choose the level of magnification by turning the nosepiece to select a lens.
5. Look through the eyepiece. You can turn the focusing knobs to lower and raise the stage, until the object is in focus.

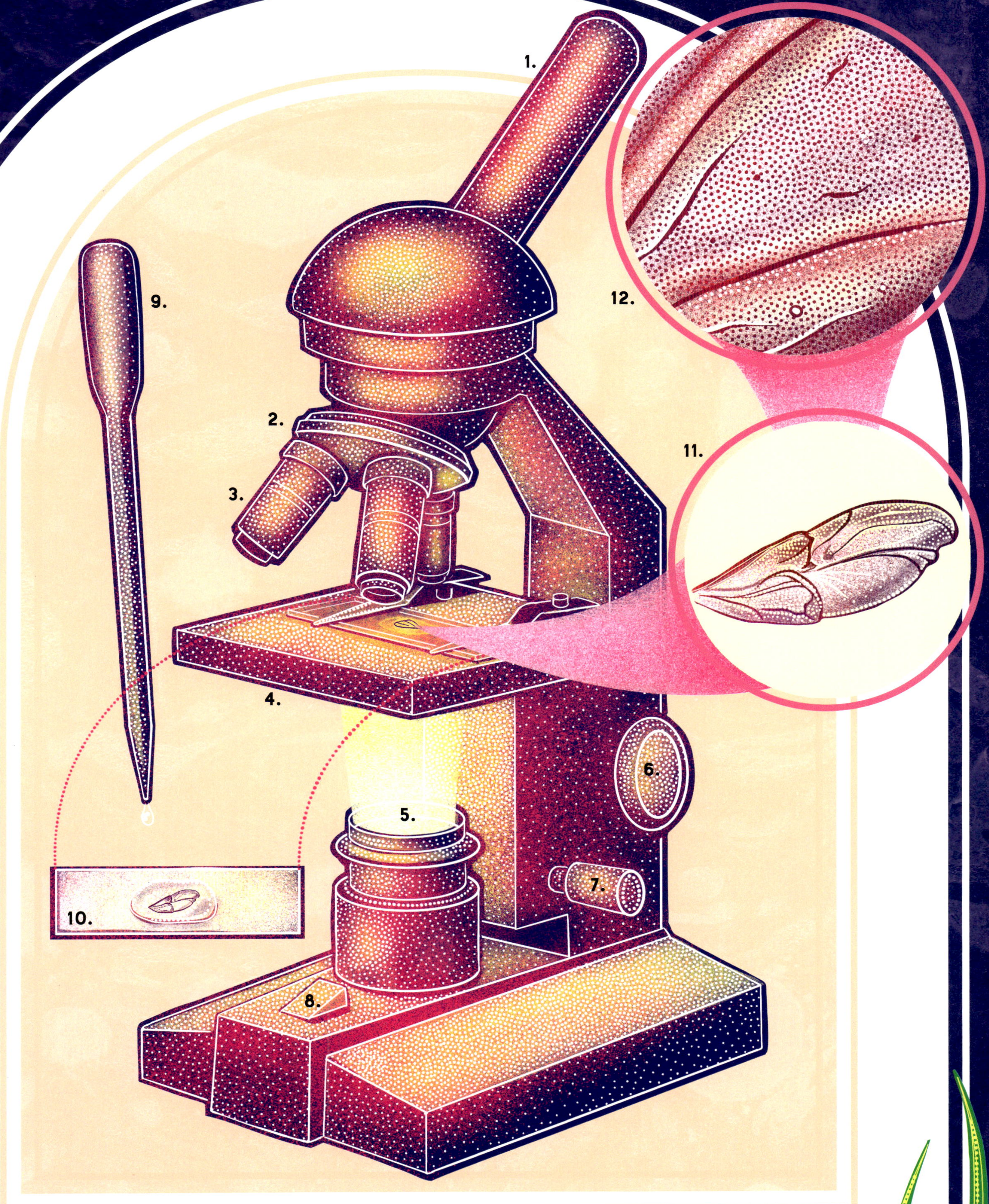

PLATE KEY

1. EYEPIECE **2.** NOSEPIECE **3.** OBJECTIVE LENS **4.** STAGE **5.** LAMP
6. COARSE FOCUS **7.** FINE FOCUS **8.** ON/OFF SWITCH **9.** PIPETTE
10. SPECIMEN SLIDE **11.** LADYBIRD WING **12.** LADYBIRD WING MAGNIFIED

THE BUILDING BLOCKS OF OUR WORLD

MICROSCOPES HELP US UNDERSTAND HOW THE WORLD WORKS.
They can reveal what things are made of and how they do what they do.

WHAT LIFE IS MADE OF

All living things – also called **organisms** – are made up of **cells**. These are the tiny building blocks of life. Living things that are made of many cells are called **multicellular** organisms. You are an example of a multicellular organism! You contain trillions of different types of cells that make up all the parts of your body and perform different functions. But some living things are only made up of one single cell. We call these **unicellular** organisms.

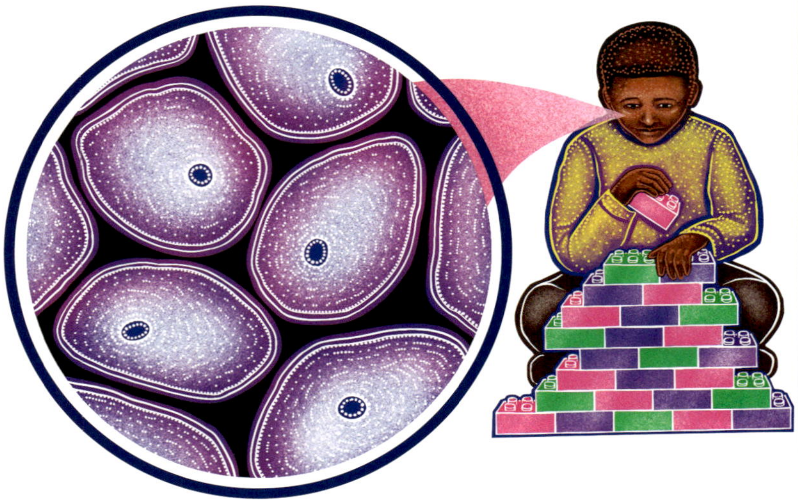

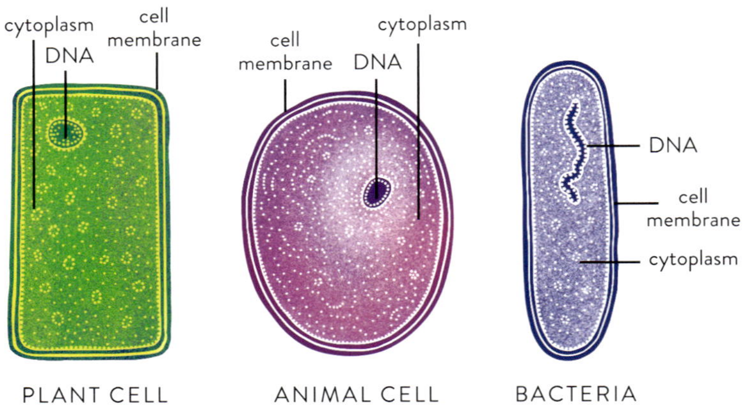

WHAT CELLS ARE MADE OF

All living cells have some structures in common. The cell membrane keeps everything all together, like the rubber skin of a water balloon. The **cytoplasm** is a jelly-like fluid inside. They all have genetic material, or DNA, which contains all the information they need to reproduce.

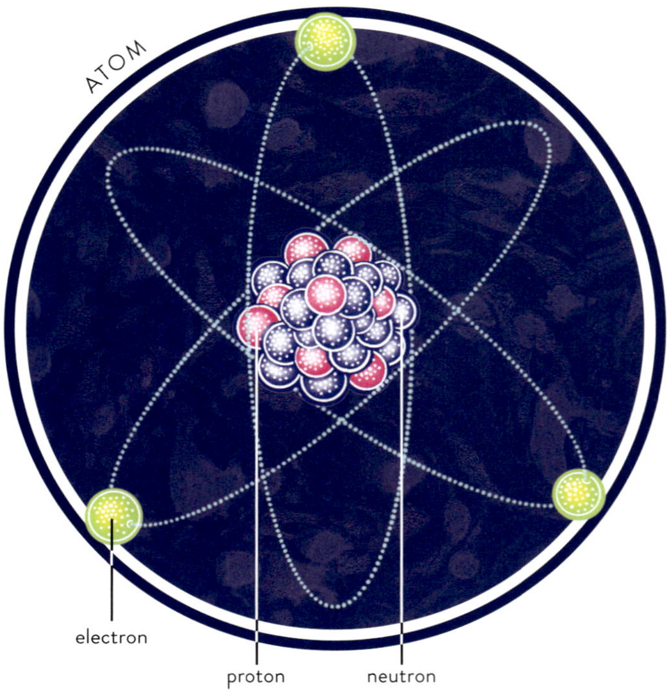

WHAT EVERYTHING IS MADE OF

Everything in the universe – including cells and all the tiny parts they are made of – are made from even smaller particles called **atoms**. Atoms are the building blocks of everything that exists. But what are they made of? Even smaller parts! They consist of a nucleus, containing protons and neutrons, and are orbited by electrons, which are even smaller.

With all these building blocks within building blocks, how much smaller could things get? Well, protons and neutrons are made up of quarks, the smallest particles of matter known to man.

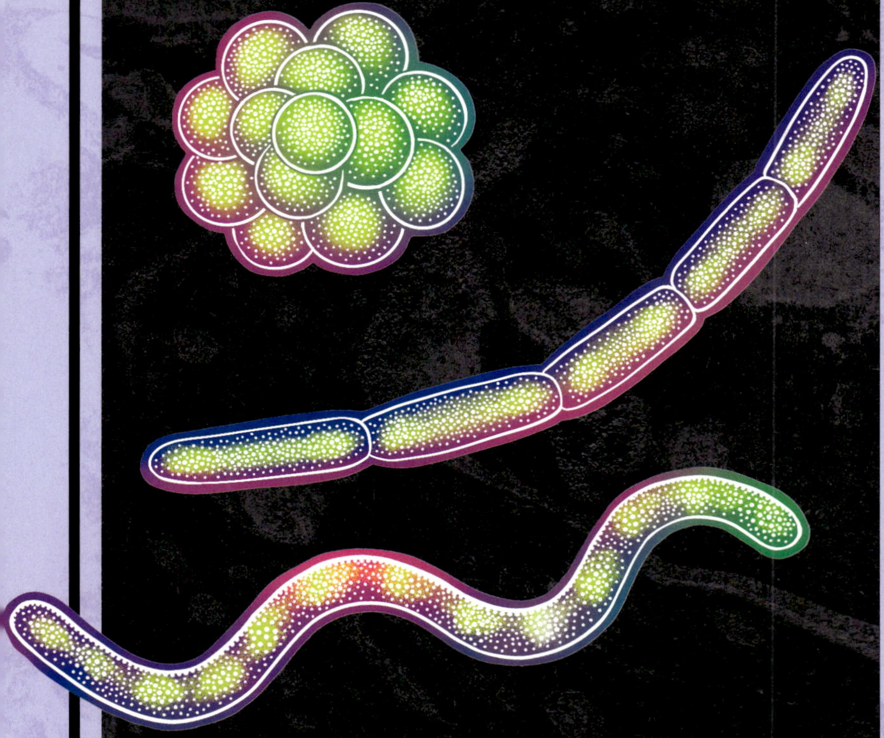

BACTERIA

Bacteria are unicellular organisms. They exist all around us and are extremely diverse. They can be harmful to humans, but they can also be helpful – in fact, they are essential to life!

PROTOZOA

Protozoa are also unicellular organisms, like bacteria. However, they are much bigger than bacteria, and are structurally more similar to animal and plant cells because they all have a nucleus containing their DNA, whereas a bacteria's DNA floats freely.

VIRUSES

Viruses are not unicellular organisms in their own right. Instead, these pirates of the microscopic world 'hijack' the living cells of other organisms, taking them over in order to make many more copies of themselves.

Though there is some debate, most scientists say that viruses can't be considered living things because they don't perform all of the life processes that other organisms do. For example, they can't grow or reproduce on their own.

IN THE GARDEN

IT'S A WARM SUMMER MORNING, A PERFECT DAY for a stroll in the garden. What microscopic wonders are waiting to be revealed?

SPIDER SPINNERETS

SILK-SPINNING SPIDERS

Ever wondered how a spider makes its web? It uses amazing organs on its bottom called spinnerets. Each spinneret has multiple spigots, which are nozzle-like structures that produce thin strands of gooey silk. The spider spins these delicate strands together into stronger, thicker thread, which quickly hardens into the stretchy fibre we know as spider's silk.

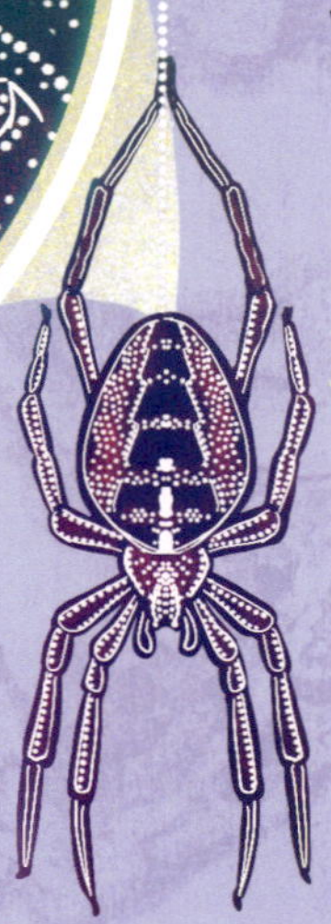

LIFE-GIVING LEAVES

What's green and helps us breathe? Chlorophyll! Put a leaf under the microscope and you'll likely see stacks of plant cells with little green bobbles inside. These are chloroplasts, which contain chlorophyll – a green pigment that absorbs energy from sunlight to make food for the plant. This process is called **photosynthesis**, and it also produces **oxygen** – a gas that we need to breathe. Plants release this oxygen into the air through little lip-like pores in their leaves, called stomata.

LEAF CELLS CONTAINING CHLOROPLASTS

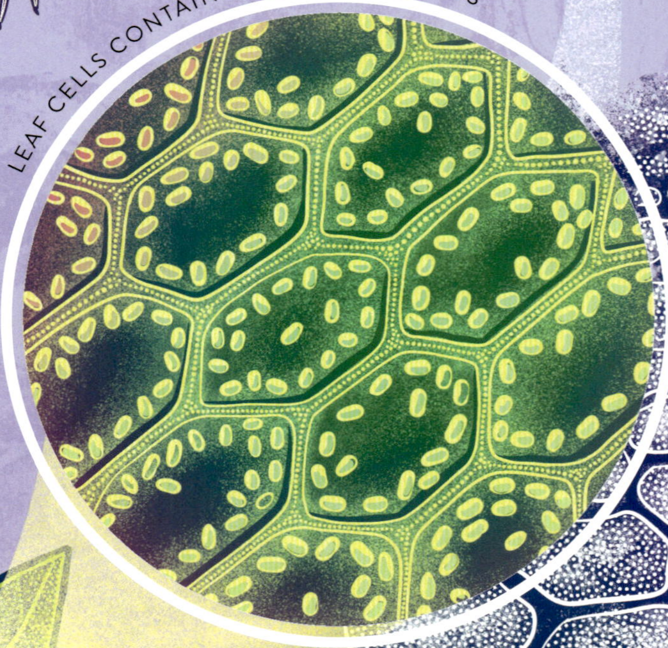

PRETTY POLLEN

Many plants produce a fine powder called pollen, which is spread to other plants so that they can produce seeds. Under the microscope, pollen can look very different depending on which plant it came from and how the pollen is transported. For example, some need to catch a ride on animals, others are blown about by the wind.

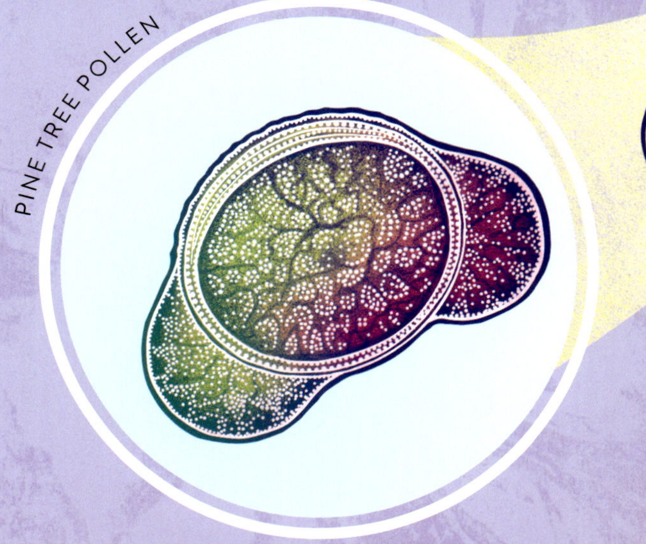

Pine tree pollen is transported by wind. It is smooth and has air sacs on the sides, which help it float better on the breeze.

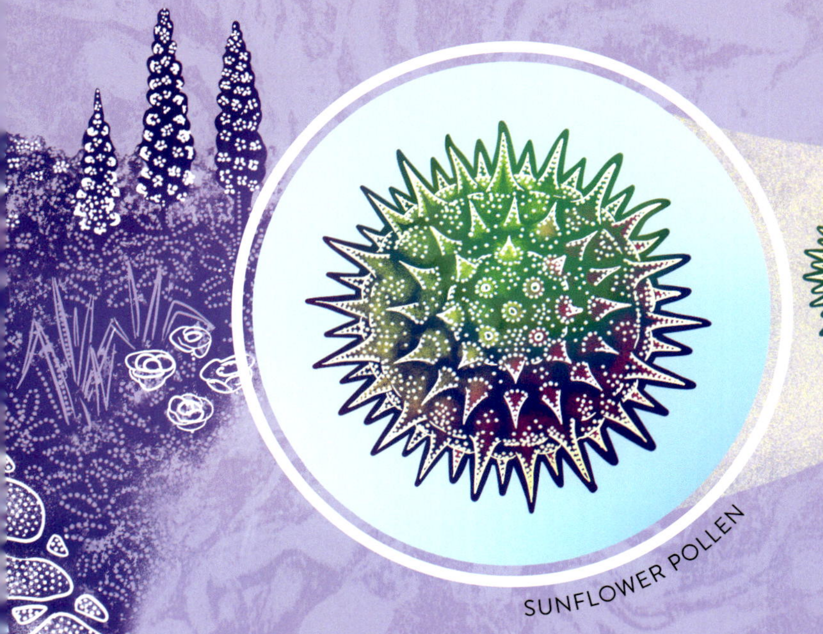

Sunflower pollen looks like spiky little balls. The spikes catch onto the furry bodies of insects, such as butterflies, who will carry the pollen on to other flowers they visit.

IN THE **POND**

ADD A PIPETTE OF POND WATER TO A SLIDE, PLACE IT UNDER a microscope and you will see that it's bustling with minute life.

TODDLING TARDIGRADES

Tardigrades, or 'water bears', are **microanimals** found in every **habitat** on Earth, and have been around for at least 500 million years. Tardigrades are most famous for being excellent survivalists; able to withstand extreme temperatures and hostile conditions by slowing down all their life processes.

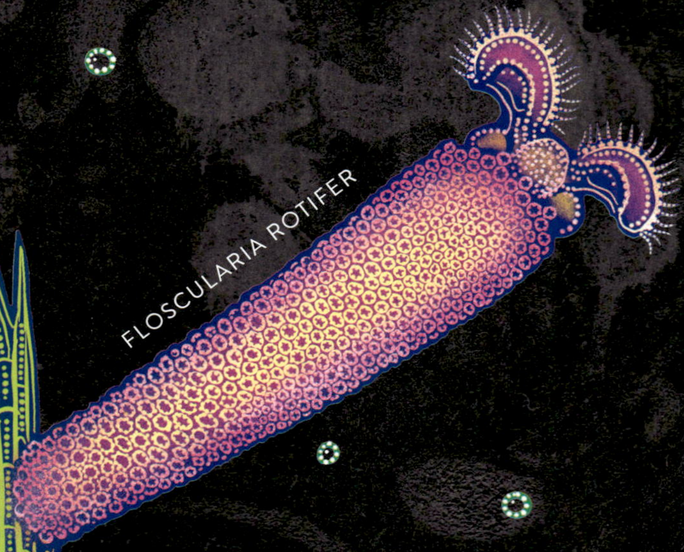

ROLLICKING ROTIFERS

Rotifers are also microanimals. There are many different types of rotifers, but they all have a corona – a crown of wiggling hairs called **cilia** which give the illusion that the corona is rotating like a wheel. This movement makes a whirlpool that sucks food into their mouths, but it can have other uses too. For example, *Floscularia* are a type of rotifer that build tube homes for themselves, using their cilia like a cement mixer to shape 'bricks' out of mud and debris.

DANCING DAPHNIA

Daphnia are commonly known as 'water fleas' because they look and jump around a bit like the itchy fleas that nibble our pets. Their transparent shell means that under the microscope you can see their heart beating. You can sometimes see clusters of round eggs growing inside female daphnia. The eggs hatch inside the female and she gives birth to live young.

PLATE KEY

1. HYDRA tentacled microanimals with an amazing ability to grow back damaged limbs. **2.** CYCLOPS named for their singular eye spot, just like the one-eyed creatures from Greek mythology. **3.** AMOEBA a shape-shifting, unicellular organism that engulfs its food into its jelly-like body. **4.** DESMID a highly symmetrical type of green **algae**. **5.** STENTOR unicellular organisms that attach themselves to pond plants or other surfaces, and suck food into their mouth by creating currents with their cilia. **6.** VOLVOX a type of green algae.

IN THE **FOREST**

YOU'RE WALKING IN A FOREST, ADMIRING THE LICHEN-COVERED TREES. Mushrooms have sprouted from old, dead branches on the ground. Out of the corner of your eye, you spot a deer grazing. Forests are teeming with different kinds of life, but much of it remains hidden, too small to see with the naked eye.

TREE DWELLERS

A tree is not just a tree. The wood of an average living tree contains more than 1 trillion **microorganisms** – one for every 20 tree cells! The type of microorganisms that you might find depends on the kind of tree. For example, maple trees, known for producing sap that gets turned into syrup, are host to a lot of sugar-eating microorganisms, such as penicillium.

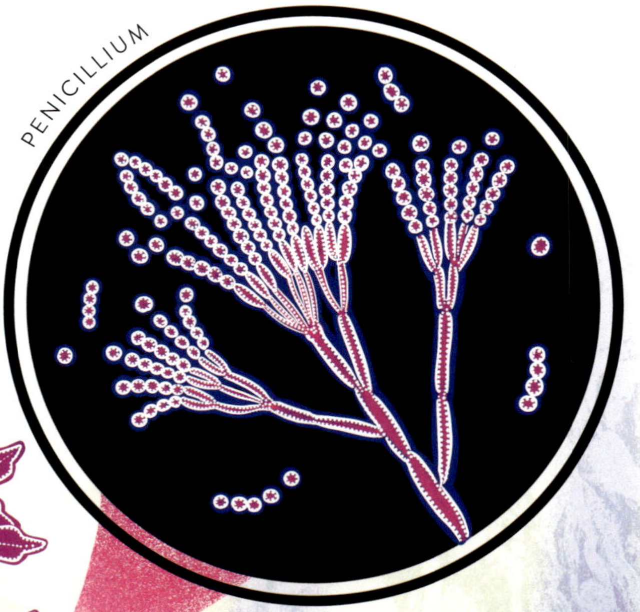

SPREADING SPORES

Spores are tiny reproductive cells produced by **fungi** and some plants, such as ferns and mosses. Like plant seeds, they are released and spread – often by wind, rain or animals – before growing into new fungi or plants.

MAKING MUSHROOMS

Most mushrooms have gills or pores under their caps where their spores are released from. Once in their new location, the spores **germinate** into tiny, root-like threads called hyphae, which stretch out into the soil, or other decaying matter. From these, the **fruiting body** of a mushroom will grow.

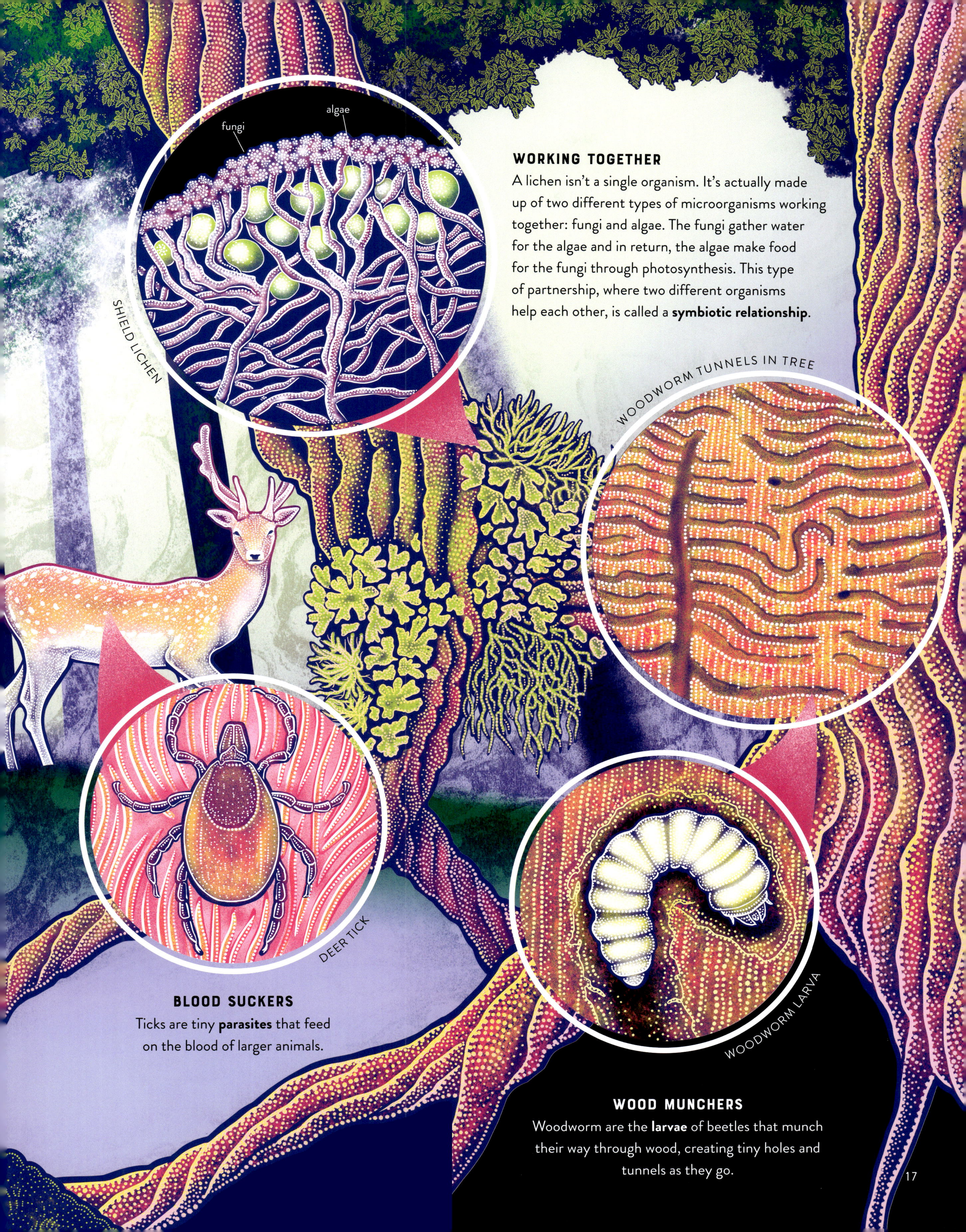

WORKING TOGETHER

A lichen isn't a single organism. It's actually made up of two different types of microorganisms working together: fungi and algae. The fungi gather water for the algae and in return, the algae make food for the fungi through photosynthesis. This type of partnership, where two different organisms help each other, is called a **symbiotic relationship**.

BLOOD SUCKERS

Ticks are tiny **parasites** that feed on the blood of larger animals.

WOOD MUNCHERS

Woodworm are the **larvae** of beetles that munch their way through wood, creating tiny holes and tunnels as they go.

IN THE **SOIL**

YOU'RE VOLUNTEERING AT THE LOCAL PARK, PLANTING BULBS IN THE RICH, BROWN SOIL. The dirt gets all over your hands and under your fingernails! Soil might seem like it's just 'dirt', but it's actually full of essential microscopic workers that are busy making life possible.

MINI RECYCLERS

Soil contains creatures that break down and decompose organic material, such as the remains of dead plants and animals, turning them into **nutrients** for new plants and other organisms to grow.

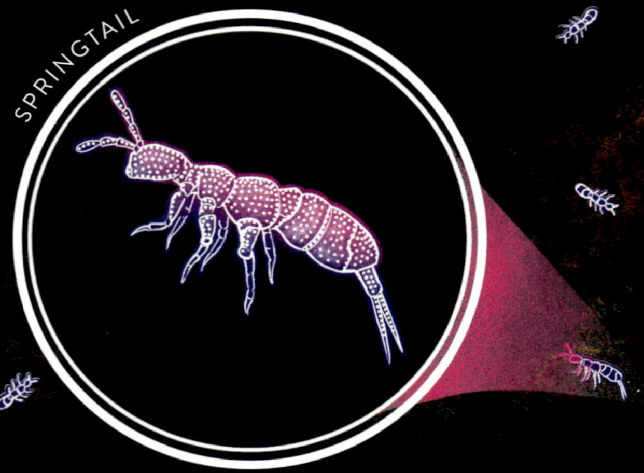

SUPER SPRINGERS

Springtails are tiny insect-like creatures, about 1-2 mm long. They eat dead and rotting material in the soil, helping to break it down in the process. They can jump hundreds of times their own body length.

NIFTY NEMATODES

Nematodes are microscopic worms. They are tiny **predators** that eat bacteria and fungi, which helps to put nutrients back into the soil.

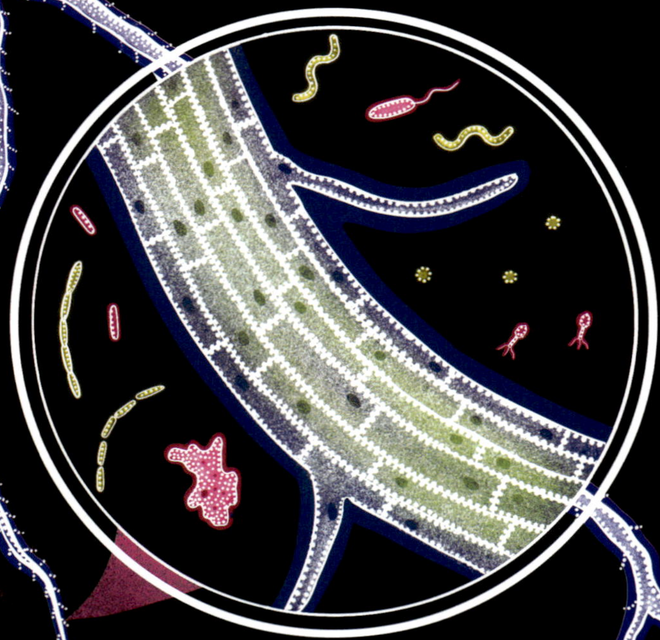

ROOTING FOR YOU

The area of soil that surrounds a plant's roots is called a **rhizosphere**. It is usually packed with a team of microorganisms that form a symbiotic relationship with the plant. The microorganisms help the plant roots absorb nutrients and in return, the plants provide them with **carbon**, which gives them energy.

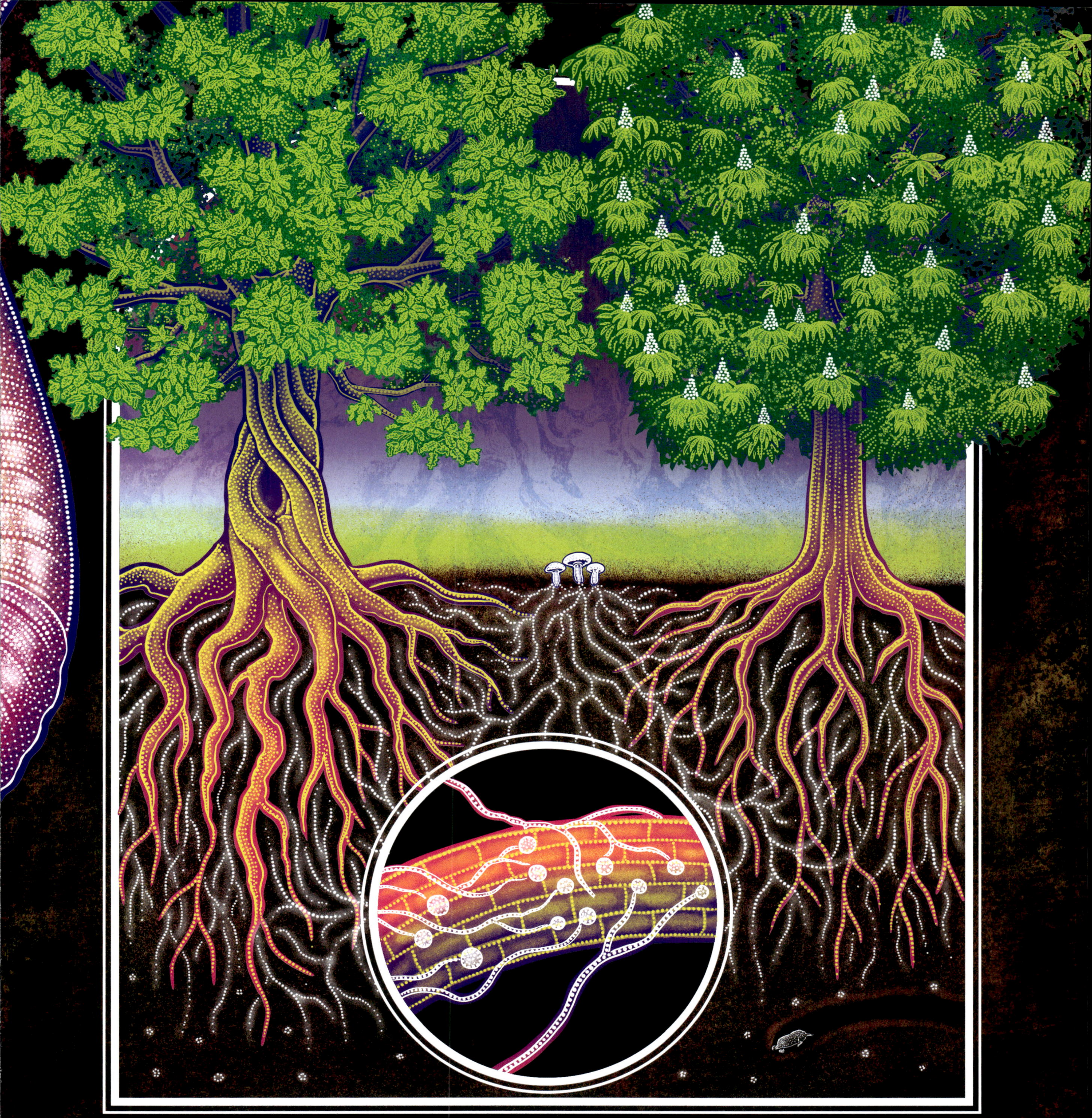

FUNGAL NETWORKS

Mycorrhizal fungi pass nutrients and water to the roots of plants. The fungi have a more extensive network in the soil, reaching much further than the plant's own roots. In turn, the plant provides them with access to food created through photosynthesis. Sometimes these mycorrhizal networks connect to those of other plants. For example, some herbs use these networks to steal sugars from trees instead of making their own!

ON THE **BEACH**

YOU'RE AT THE BEACH, MAKING A SANDCASTLE.

You pack as much sand as you can into your bucket and brush tiny grains off your knees as you stand. You wonder how many grains of sand there must be in your bucket right now.

SEEING SAND

If you scooped out a cubic metre of beach sand and counted all the grains, you would reach around 8 billion! That's close to the total number of people on Earth, and – just like people – every grain of sand is unique. But what are they made of?

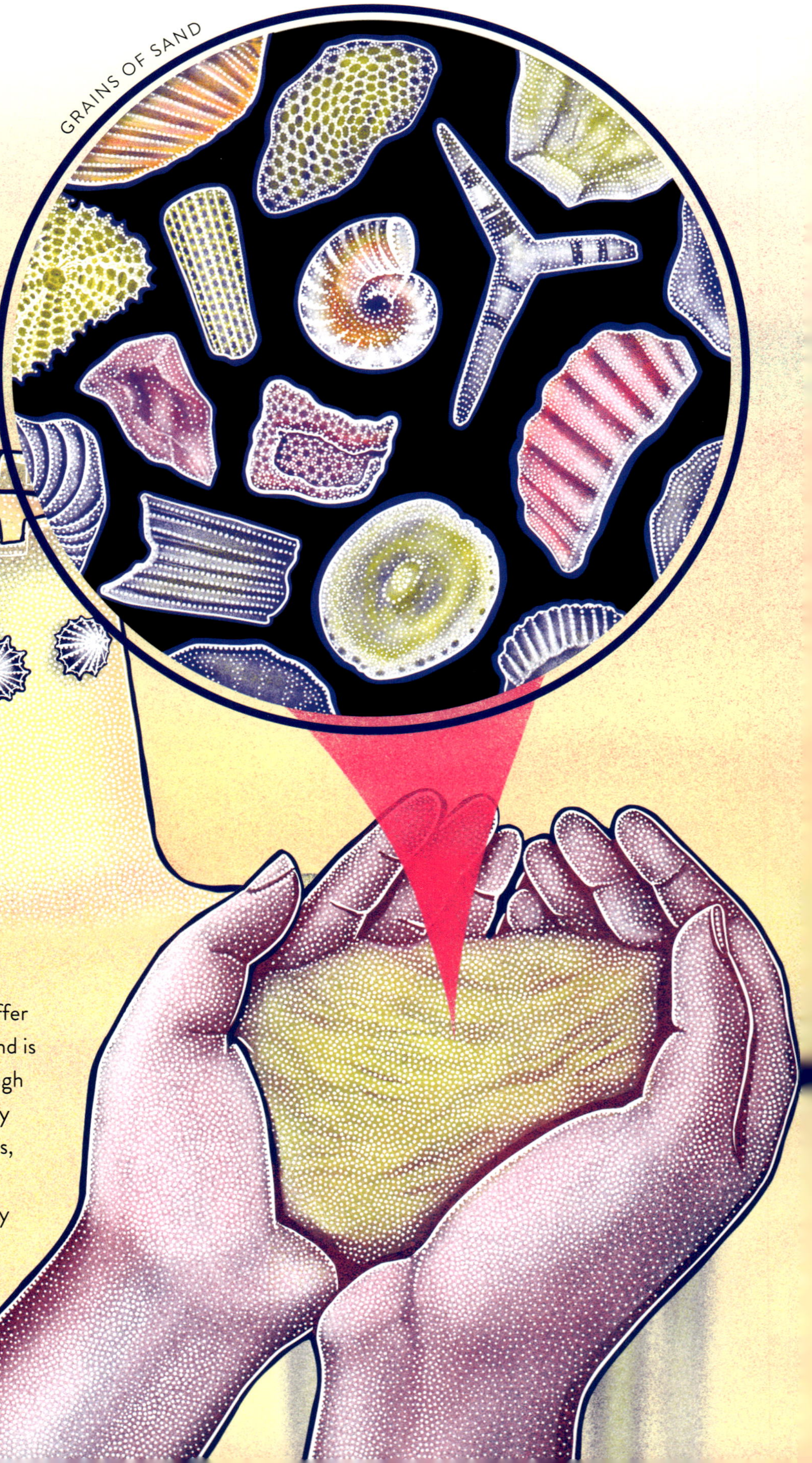

MULTI-GRAINS

You might have noticed that grains of sand usually differ in colour, even on the same beach. This is because sand is made from lots of different things. It is created through **erosion** – the process of materials being worn away by water, wind and other forces. Different hard materials, such as rock, coral and shells, are broken down into smaller parts and moved from one place to another by these natural forces. The broken bits of materials get smaller and smaller as they continue to wear away over time, ending up as tiny grains of sand.

MINI CRYSTALS

Hard **minerals** within rock take much longer to erode than softer materials, which break down more easily. This means that hard minerals, such as tiny pieces of quartz – a common kind of **crystal** – are often found in sand.

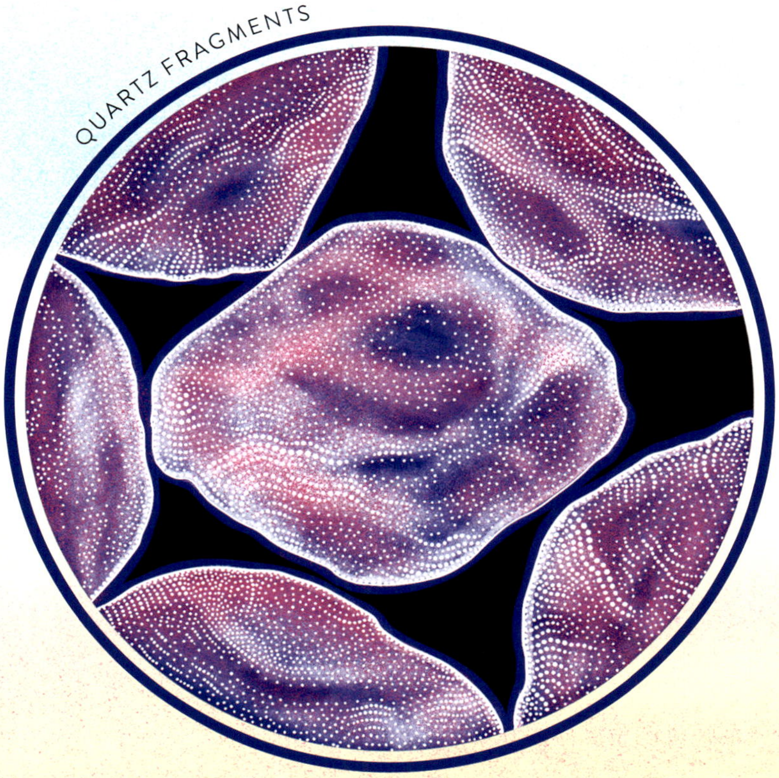

TINY SHELLS

Some beach sand includes tiny, fossilised shells of unicellular organisms called foraminifera. Some of these shells are millions of years old – some even date back to before the time of dinosaurs! By analysing sand under a microscope, we can find out more information about the sea life that lives, or used to live, in the area.

FISH POO

Sand can also be made from fish poo! Parrotfish use their hard beaks to scrape the algae off coral, taking some of the coral with it. They then poop out the hard coral fragments, which they can't digest. This creates beautiful white beaches.

IN THE OCEAN

YOU ARE LOOKING AT THE SEA ON A STORMY DAY. LARGE WAVES SWELL AND CRASH into white foam. The water stretches off into the distance, meeting the thunderous sky on the horizon. You are awed by the immense size and power of the ocean. It is home to blue whales – the largest creatures in the world – but most **marine** life is too small to see without a microscope.

TINY DRIFTERS

Plankton is a very broad name given to marine organisms that are not big or strong enough to swim against ocean currents and tides, so they drift with them instead. Most plankton are microscopic. There are two main types of plankton: phytoplankton and zooplankton.

DIATOMS

SEA BUTTERFLY

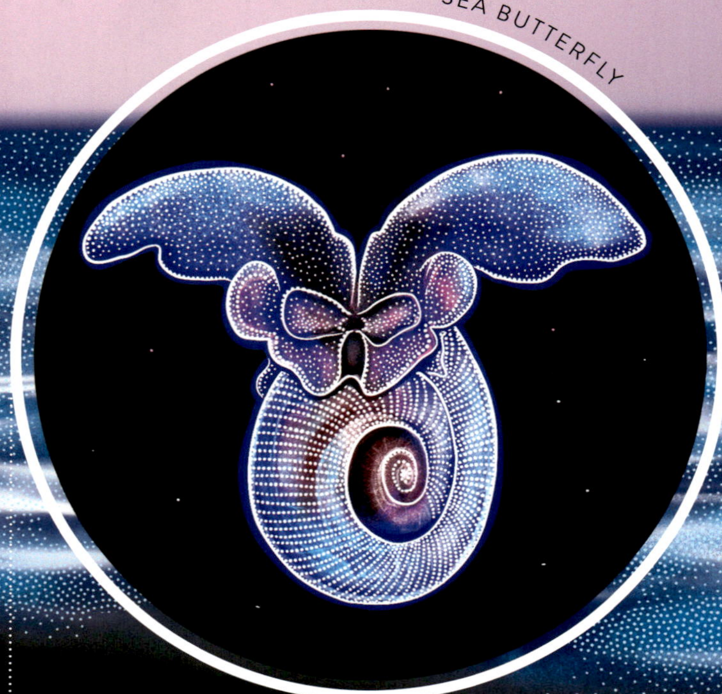

PHYTOPLANKTON

Phytoplankton are a group of plant-like microorganisms. Just like plants on land, phytoplankton make their own energy through photosynthesis. More than half of the oxygen we breathe comes from these tiny floaters.

Diatoms are a type of unicellular phytoplankton, known as the 'Jewels of the Sea'. This is because they take a material called silica from the water and use it to turn their outer cell wall into a hard, transparent shell, a bit like glass. These shells come in many intricate shapes and patterns, which look like tiny gems or beads.

ZOOPLANKTON

When you hear the word 'zoo', you might think of the place with lots of animals. That's because 'zoo' means 'animal' and is often used at the start of words related to them. Zooplankton are a group of tiny marine animals. Many larger animals start out life as zooplankton, such as fish eggs and crab larvae.

The zooplankton sea butterflies are tiny sea snails with wing-like flaps on their feet, which they use to elegantly 'fly' through the water. They are rarely bigger than 1 cm when fully grown, and their shells are thinner than a human hair.

PLATE KEY

1. *TRIPOS MUELLERI* a dinoflagellate, which is a type of unicellular phytoplankton. **2.** *CHAETOCEROS DEBILIS* a colony of diatoms that form a spiral. **3.** *MERISMOPEDIA AFFIXA* a type of **cyanobacteria** that form neat rows in a colony. **4.** CLAM LARVA clams grow hard shells in their adult forms and settle on the sea floor, but their larvae free float in the ocean. **5.** FISH EGG **6.** GREEN CRAB LARVA this is an early larval form of a crab called the zoea stage. **7.** GREEN CRAB LARVA this more developed larval form, which comes after the zoea form, is called the megalops stage. **8.** COMMON STARFISH LARVA this is the brachiolaria larval stage of a starfish.

IN OUR HOMES

IT'S RAINING OUTSIDE, AND YOU JUST GOT HOME.

You take off your coat and shoes, and get into comfy clothes before snuggling under a blanket with your favourite book. Our homes are the places we feel most familiar with, but there's a hidden world that looks much more unfamiliar!

FUZZY FOOD

You might notice that when food is accidentally left out, or goes uneaten for too long, it can turn fuzzy. This fuzz is mould – a type of fungus – and it doesn't just appear from nowhere. Even in the cleanest home, mould spores float around in the air. When they land on something full of nutrients, like food, the spores will germinate and grow into mould. Harmful bacteria can also grow on food left out. It's important to store food properly, as spoiled food can make you ill.

However, not all moulds and bacteria are bad. Throughout history we've used these microorganisms to make food. Certain cheeses, yoghurt and bread are all examples of food made using bacteria and fungi.

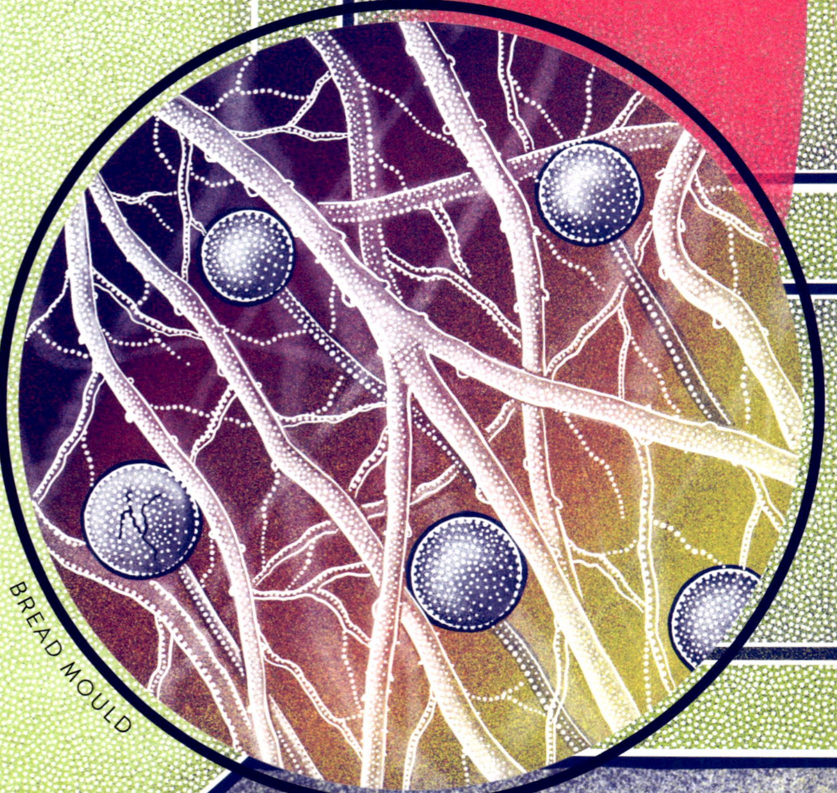

FLUFFY FIBRES

Part of what makes our homes so cosy are fabrics, like blankets. Fabrics under the microscope will usually show a lattice of fibres, beautifully woven together. These can be woven in different ways for different uses. The fibres of a coat are usually more tightly woven together, to help make it more waterproof. The fibres of clothing, bedding and blankets will usually be looser, to let more air pass through, making them more comfortable against the skin.

OUR UNSEEN ROOMMATES

You may have seen dust gather in corners of your home. This dust is made up of things like loose fabric fibres, dead skin flakes, pet fur and pollen. Dust mites are microscopic **arachnids** that feed on this dust. A certain amount of dust mites in the home is inevitable and they're mostly harmless, but too many can trigger allergic reactions, such as a runny nose or itching, and they can make someone's asthma worse. But don't worry, that's what dusters and vacuum cleaners are for!

IN THE **ARCTIC**

THE COLDEST PLACES ON EARTH ARE AROUND THE NORTH AND SOUTH POLES. The lowest naturally occurring temperature was recorded in the South Pole, at a teeth chattering -89°C! What can a microscope tell us about such an extreme environment?

INTRICATE SNOWFLAKES

Snowflakes are known for their unique and intricate patterns – it is often said that no two snowflakes are the same, though this would be very hard to prove! However, one thing they have in common is that they tend to have six points. This is because as water freezes, its **molecules** form a hexagonal lattice. The ice crystals then form beautiful patterns from this basic shape. Snowflakes usually form around particles in the **atmosphere**, such as ash, pollen and dust, and gas bubbles can get trapped inside them.

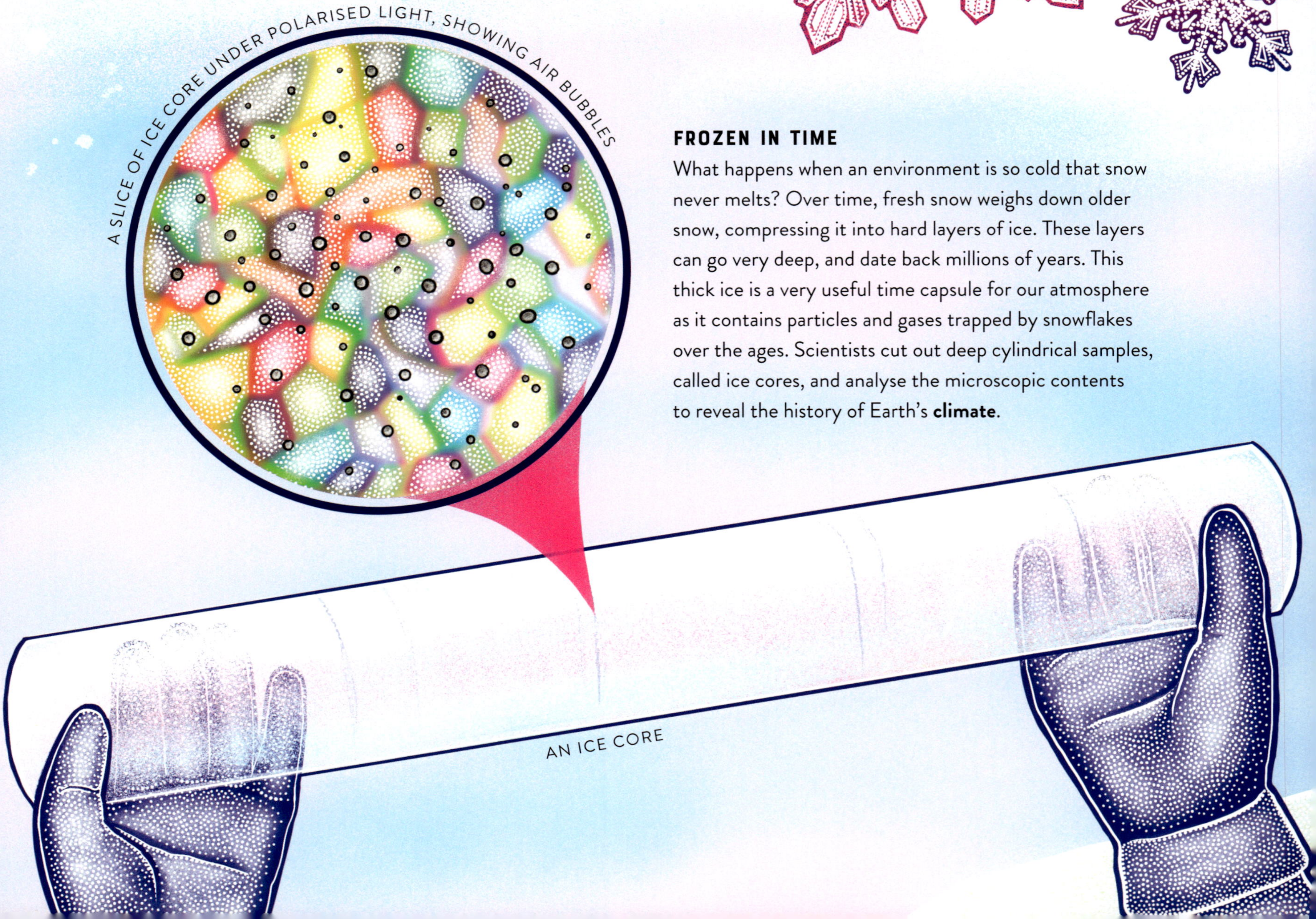

FROZEN IN TIME

What happens when an environment is so cold that snow never melts? Over time, fresh snow weighs down older snow, compressing it into hard layers of ice. These layers can go very deep, and date back millions of years. This thick ice is a very useful time capsule for our atmosphere as it contains particles and gases trapped by snowflakes over the ages. Scientists cut out deep cylindrical samples, called ice cores, and analyse the microscopic contents to reveal the history of Earth's **climate**.

LIFE FINDS A WAY

As you can imagine, extreme cold can be quite inhospitable to life, however there are many special creatures that have adapted to these harsh environments. Polar bears might look white, but a sample of their fur shows the hairs are actually transparent, reflecting the light to help them blend in with the snow. Their hairs also have a hollow core, which traps their body heat more efficiently.

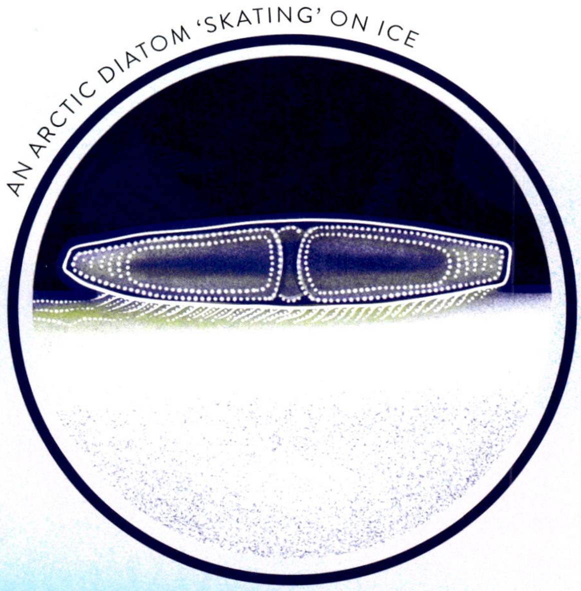

I LOVE THE COLD

Microorganisms are more able to withstand extreme temperatures than larger organisms, and many are specially adapted for cold environments. These are called psychrophiles, which means 'cold-loving'. They are able to make substances to prevent themselves from freezing.

Arctic diatoms are psychrophiles that are able to function normally at temperatures as low as -15°C. They glide along the ice using a combination of mucus and microscopic filaments that run down the centre of their body.

DID YOU KNOW?

Sometimes you can find colourful snow in the Arctic and Antarctica. The colour comes from different kinds of algae living in it.

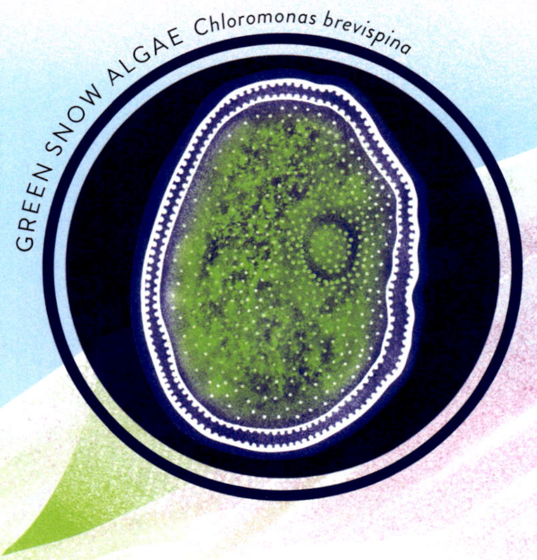

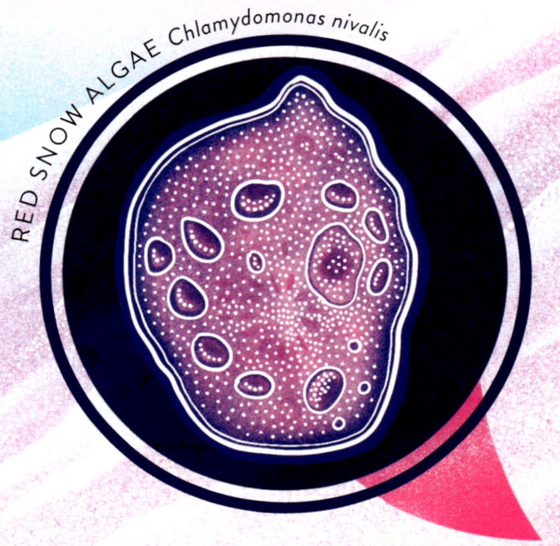

IN THE **DESERT**

YOU ARE WALKING IN THE SONORAN DESERT IN MEXICO. THE SUN BEATS DOWN on your shoulders. It's unbearably hot and dry, but somehow life continues to survive out here. Cacti tower above you, thriving despite the extreme heat. But what's going on at a microscopic level?

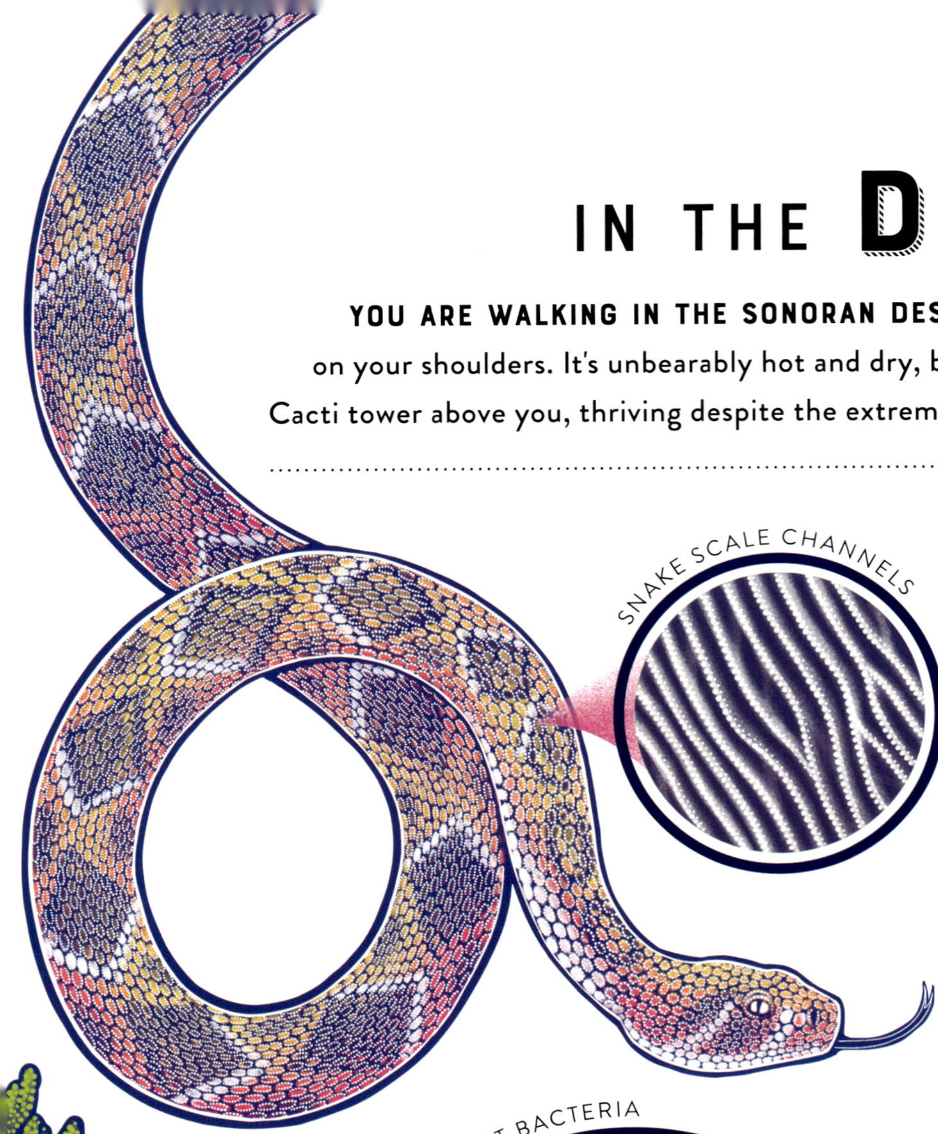

SIPPING FROM SKIN

The scales of desert snakes are covered in microscopic channels that collect rainwater and funnel it directly into their skin. This allows snakes to get the water they need directly from the sky, rather than spending time and energy finding a watering hole to drink from.

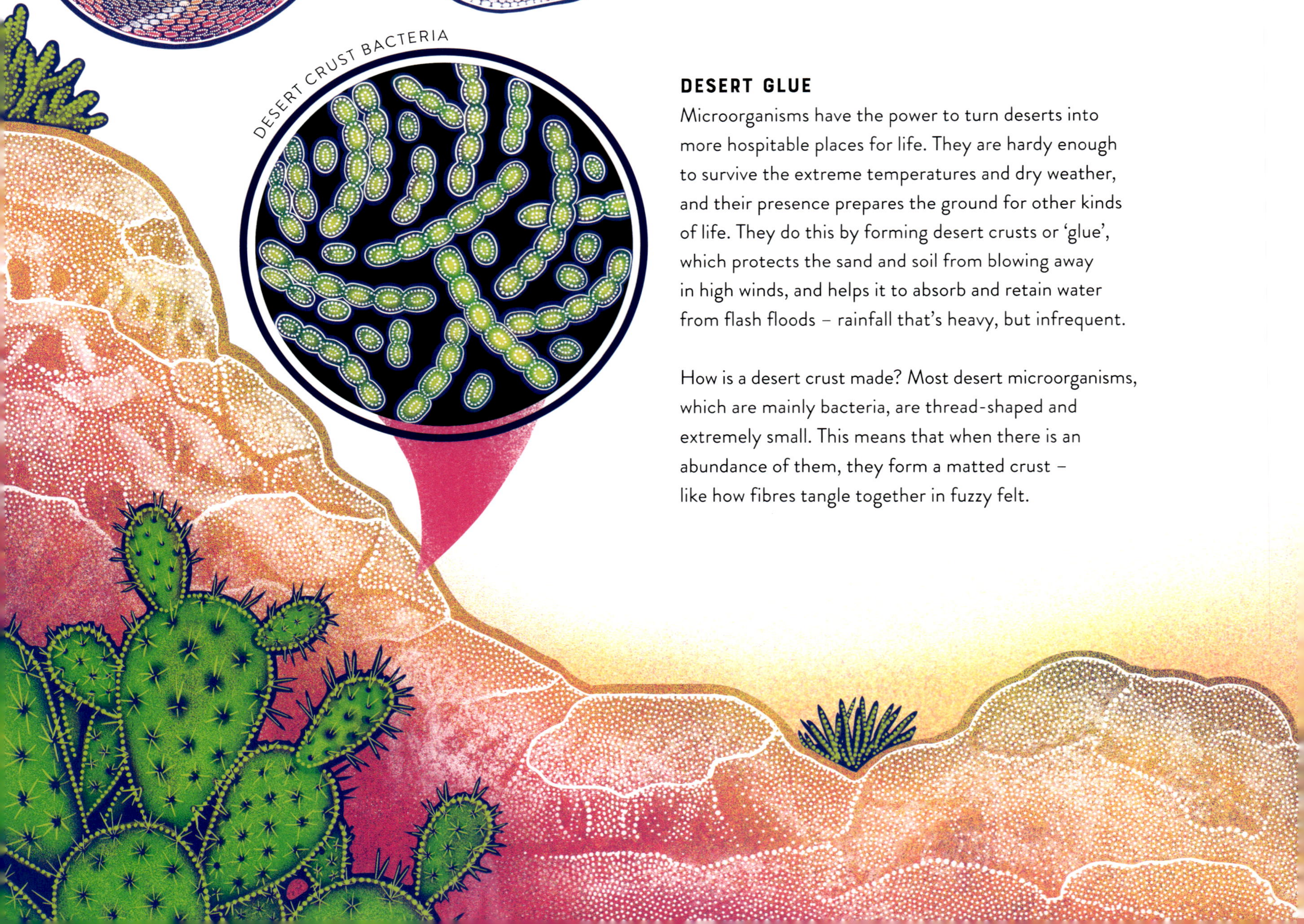

DESERT GLUE

Microorganisms have the power to turn deserts into more hospitable places for life. They are hardy enough to survive the extreme temperatures and dry weather, and their presence prepares the ground for other kinds of life. They do this by forming desert crusts or 'glue', which protects the sand and soil from blowing away in high winds, and helps it to absorb and retain water from flash floods – rainfall that's heavy, but infrequent.

How is a desert crust made? Most desert microorganisms, which are mainly bacteria, are thread-shaped and extremely small. This means that when there is an abundance of them, they form a matted crust – like how fibres tangle together in fuzzy felt.

PLATE KEY

1. SAGUARO CACTUS a giant type of cactus that can grow over 12 metres tall. **2. PARENCHYMA** are a type of specialised cactus cell that can swell in order to store water. **3. CACTUS CRYSTALS** saguaro cacti turn carbon from the air and calcium from the soil into microscopic crystals. These crystals make them less appealing to animals that might try to eat them. **4. PRICKLY PEAR CACTI** have microscopic spines going in the opposite direction, making them harder to remove, and more painful when you do.

IN OUTER SPACE

WHEN YOU THINK OF ALIENS, YOU MIGHT THINK OF LITTLE GREEN MEN IN A SPACESHIP, but if life has occurred on other planets, it would likely be much smaller than you might imagine!

TEENY TINY ALIENS

If extraterrestrial life exists, it is likely to be in the form of simple microorganisms. This is because microscopic life is more able to withstand great environmental challenges, such as extreme heat, cold and even the **vacuum** of space! Most planets don't have the perfect conditions for complex life like Earth does, but some might be hospitable enough for hardier microorganisms.

Evidence suggests that all life on Earth started with unicellular organisms, and for most of Earth's 4.5 billion year history, they were the only kind of life present. Earth used to be more like other planets. It didn't have a breathable atmosphere until microorganisms released oxygen through photosynthesis. This means that if we were to ever find life on other planets, most likely, it would be similar to an earlier stage of Earth's history.

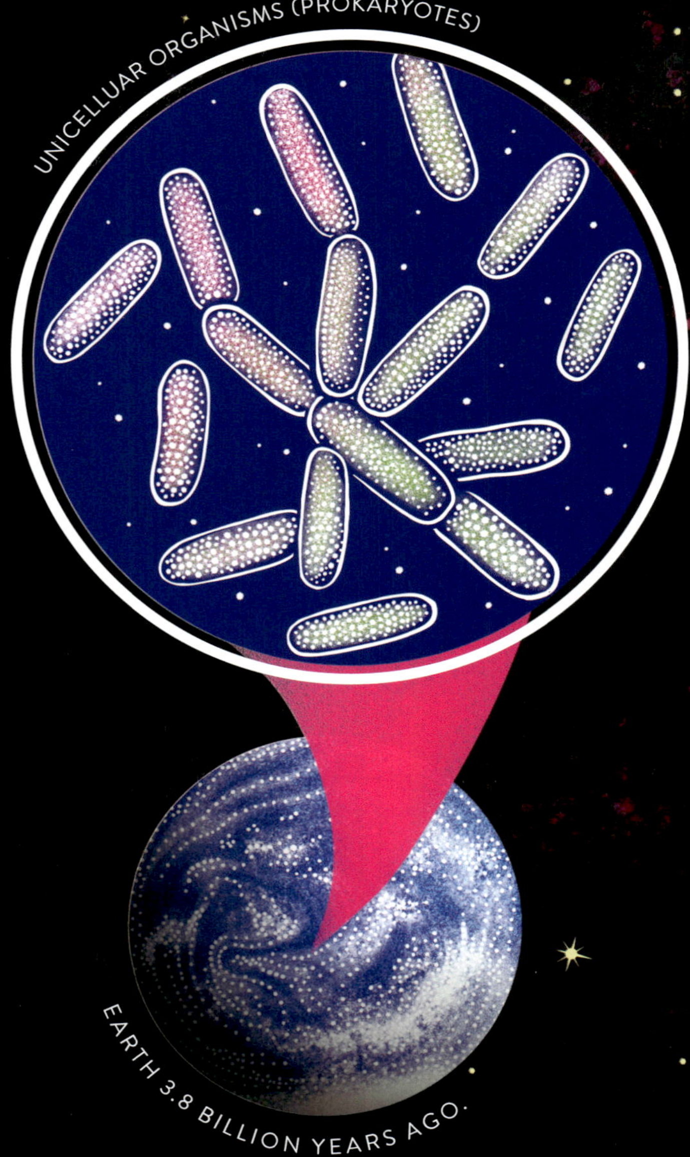

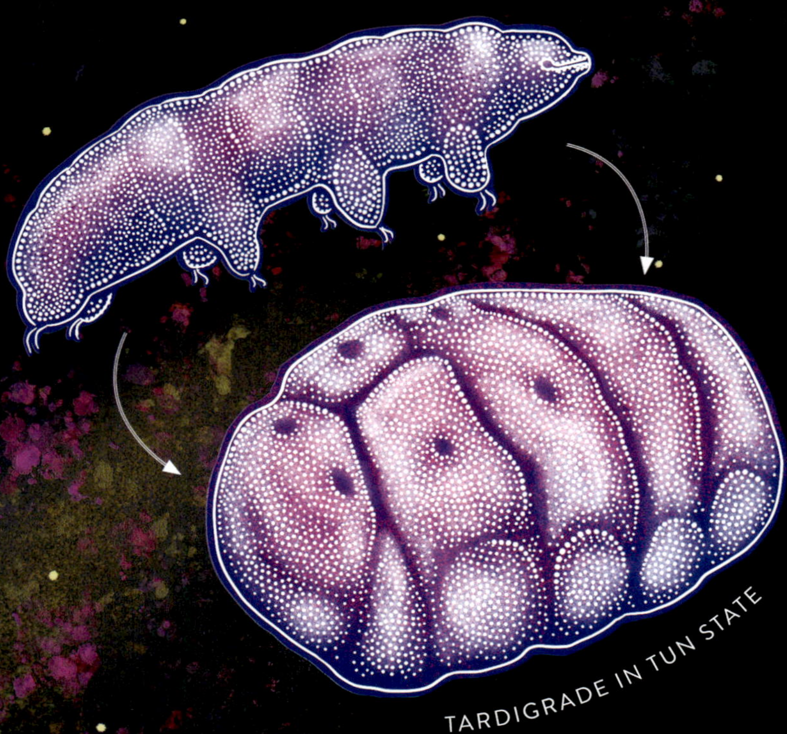

THE TINIEST ASTRONAUTS

Tardigrades are famous for being able to survive harsh conditions, but did you know that they have been sent to space? They were able to survive the vacuum and harmful cosmic radiation of space that would instantly kill a human astronaut. They do this by going into their protective 'tun' state. This is where they shrivel up, retract their limbs and slow their life processes down so much that they are close to stopping completely. They can survive decades of harsh conditions in this state.

SPACE ROCKS

You can learn a lot from rocks! Much of the research from space missions so far has centered around rock samples. In fact, the first men on the Moon, Neil Armstrong and Buzz Aldrin, didn't just wave to the camera – they also collected around 21.5 kg of Moon rock to be analysed. The samples helped scientists understand what the Moon is made of, how it likely formed and – greater still – how our solar system may have formed.

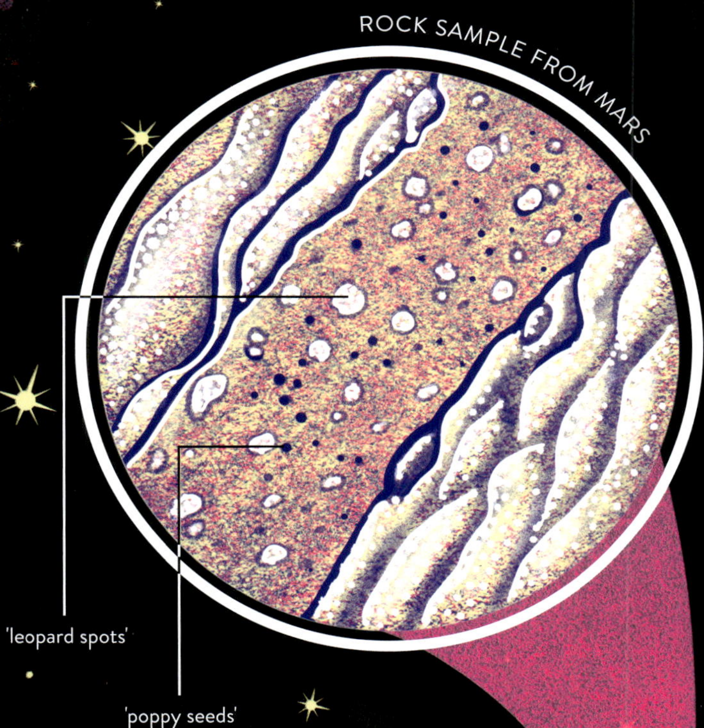

LIFE ON MARS?

We've long wondered whether Earth is the only planet to have ever had life on it. However, in 2025, scientists discovered exciting evidence that there might have been microbial life on Mars billions of years ago. A rock sample discovered by NASA's Perseverance rover, shows interesting markings – nicknamed 'leopard spots' and 'poppy seeds' – which are believed to contain minerals that are a sign of chemical reactions that could have been created by microorganisms. It's the most compelling evidence ever found that Mars may once have had life on it too!

THE HISTORY OF LENSES

THE MICROSCOPIC WORLD WAS A POWERFUL HIDDEN FORCE FOR MOST OF HISTORY.

From ancient crystal lenses, to the incredibly powerful microscopes of today. How did we get here?

STARING STATUES

AROUND 2620 TO 1334 BCE

Lenses in ancient times weren't clear enough to be used as magnifiers, but people did notice how light interacted with them in special ways.

Ancient Egyptians polished crystals into lenses and used them in the eyes of their statues. The lenses would bend the light so that the statues' eyes seemed to follow you around the room!

FIRESTARTERS

AROUND 400 BCE

Curved lenses can be used to concentrate sunlight into one spot, heating it up very rapidly. In ancient times this was very useful for creating fires. The ancient Greeks also used them as surgical tools – not to magnify, but to seal wounds with heat. We still do this today with other tools; it's called cauterisation.

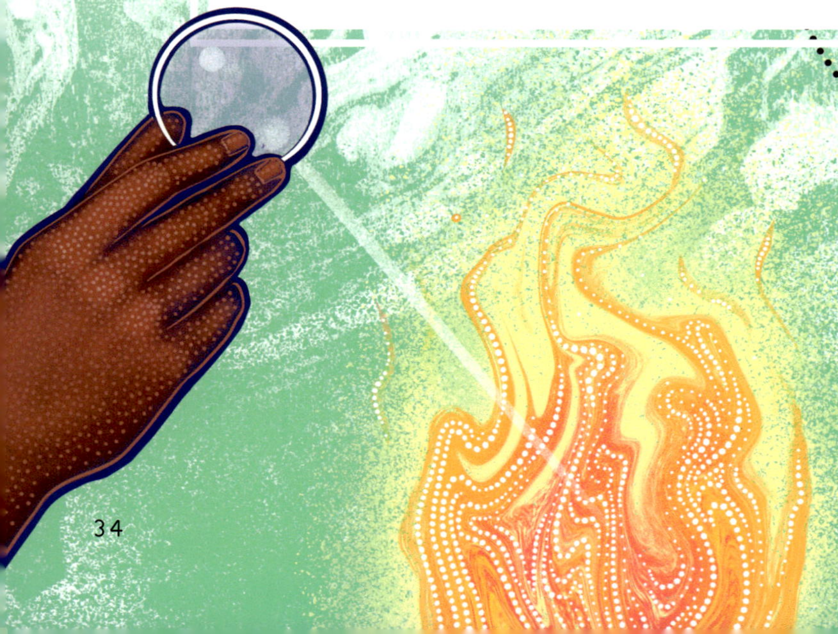

READING ROMANS

AROUND 1 CE

The Romans, who developed the art of glass blowing, used spherical glass 'reading stones' to magnify text.

A VISION VISIONARY

AROUND 1011 TO 1021 CE

Arab scholar Ibn al-Haytham published the *Book of Optics*, which suggested a theory for the science behind how light and eyes work that was incredibly accurate for its time. His work was hugely influential in the development of lenses.

GLORIOUS GLASSES

AROUND 1250S TO 1300 CE

Wearable lenses to correct eyesight were invented in Italy. Spectacles were a life-changing invention for many people who struggled with their sight.

THE MORE THE MERRIER

AROUND 1600 CE

Dutch spectacle-maker Hans Lippershey and his teenage son Zaccharias Hanssen discovered that when more lenses are used together, you can increase the magnification. They are often credited as inventing the first **compound microscope**, but this is the subject of some debate.

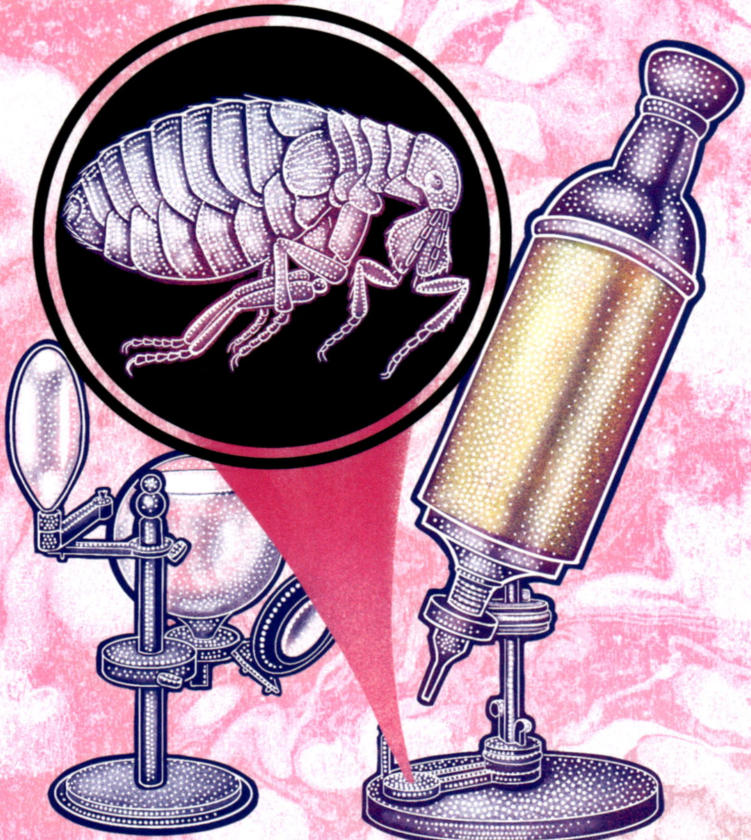

TOTALLY HOOKED

1665 CE

Robert Hooke used a microscope like this one on the left to examine all sorts of objects. He produced a large book, called *Micrographia*, about his observations, which had beautiful illustrations and became a bestseller. He was the first person to use the word 'cell' for parts of living things.

BACTERIA DESCRIBED

1674 CE

Antonie van Leeuwenhoek developed the design of a hand-held microscope by experimenting with new ways to shape lenses for higher magnification and clearer images. He managed to make lenses that could possibly magnify up to 500 times! He was the first to describe bacteria with his creation, from a sample of lake water.

SUSPICIONS ABOUT DISEASE

1800S CE

Links started being made between microorganisms and disease. In 1830, Joseph Lister made microscopes that produced much clearer images, and his son (also called Joseph) used these to investigate how wounds became infected.

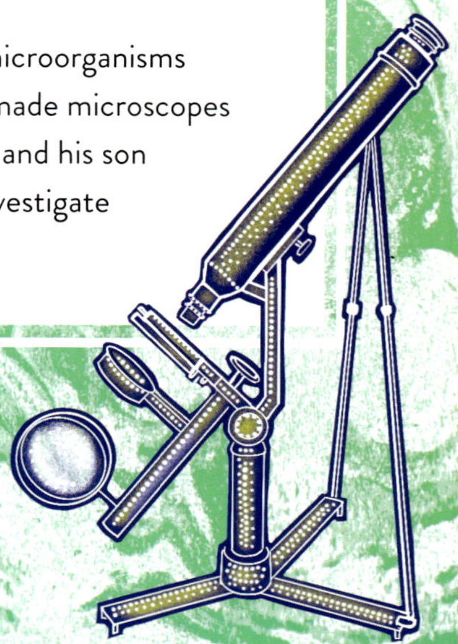

GERM THEORY GERMINATES

1861 CE

Finally, in 1861, French scientist Louis Pasteur published his findings on 'Germ Theory'. He was able to disprove the old belief that living organisms could arise from non-living matter, and he showed that microorganisms were responsible for infectious diseases. This knowledge has saved countless lives.

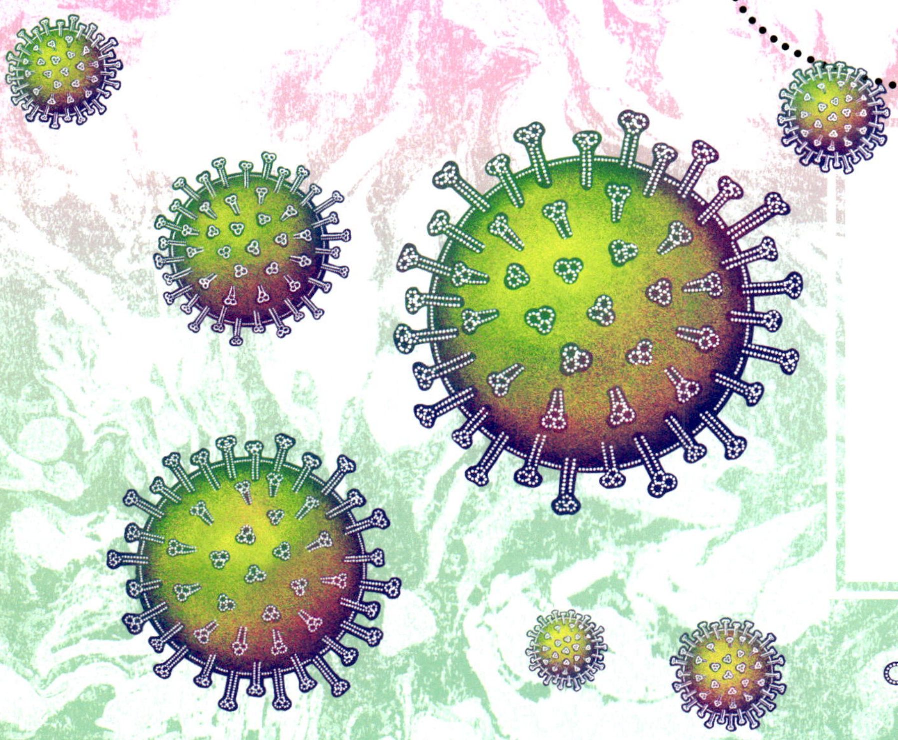

VIRUSES VISUALISED

1631 CE

In 1931, the first electron microscope was developed by German scientists Ernst Ruska and Max Knoll, allowing magnification up to a million times. This was another huge leap for medicine, as it allowed viruses to be seen and studied.

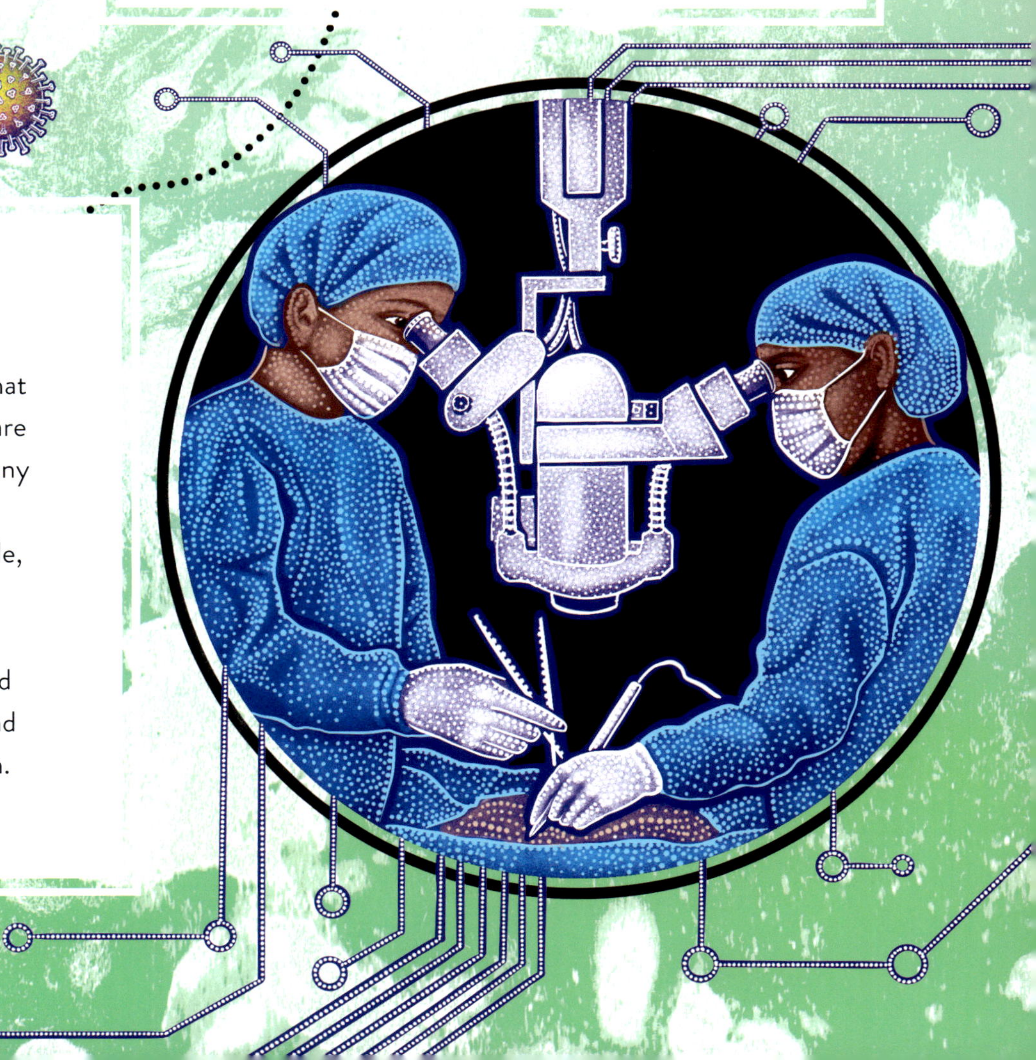

MODERN MICROSCOPES

PRESENT DAY

Today, microscopes have become so powerful that it's possible to produce images of atoms. There are over 40 different types of microscopes with many fascinating applications. They allow us to make machinery smaller than ever before. For example, the computers, smartphones and tablets in use today all work because of microchips – tiny electronic circuits. Surgery is more sophisticated than ever before, as doctors use microscopes and special tools to operate with incredible precision.

GLOSSARY

algae Small, plant-like aquatic organisms.

arachnids Member of a group of invertebrates (animals without a backbone), including spiders, scorpions and ticks, which don't have wings but do have hard exoskeletons, and almost always have eight legs.

atmosphere The gases that surround our Earth.

atoms Very small particles that are the building blocks of everything that exists.

carbon A chemical element found in all living things, as well as substances like coal and oil. It can also take the form of diamonds or graphite, and is part of a gas called carbon dioxide, found in air.

cells The tiny structures that all living things are made of.

cilia Hair-like structures that stick out of certain cells.

climate The average weather conditions in a particular location over a long period of time.

compound microscope A microscope that uses multiple lenses to magnify objects.

crystal A solid whose molecules are arranged in a repeating pattern. Many crystals are found in rocks and can have beautiful and unusual shapes.

cyanobacteria An aquatic bacteria that can photosynthesise, also known as blue-green algae.

cytoplasm A jelly-like substance that fills the inside of cells.

electrons Tiny particles that orbit the nucleus of an atom.

erosion When rock or soil is worn away and transported by natural forces, such as wind or water.

fruiting body The part of a fungus that produces spores, such as the stalk and cap of a mushroom that is visible above the surface.

fungi (plural of fungus) Plant-like organisms including mushrooms, moulds and yeasts, which produce spores and feed on organic matter.

gastrotrich Microscopic aquatic invertebrates that live in the spaces between sand grains and soil particles.

germinate The act of a seed or spore beginning to grow.

habitat The natural home of a living thing.

larvae (plural of larva) The young form of an animal before it undergoes a metamorphosis (transformation) into its adult form. Animals that have a larval stage in their life cycle include insects and many aquatic creatures, such as crab and shrimp.

lens A curved piece of glass, or other transparent material, used to make things looks larger, smaller, closer or clearer.

magnification The process of making something look bigger than it is.

marine Relating to the sea.

microanimals Animals that are too small to see with the naked eye.

microbiome The large collection of microorganisms, including bacteria, fungi and viruses, that naturally live on and inside our bodies.

microorganisms Living things that are too small to see with the naked eye.

minerals Solid natural substances found in the earth, such as metals and salts.

molecules Groups of two or more atoms chemically bonded together. They are the smallest unit of a substance that can exist by itself and still have the properties of that substance. For example, water molecules are the smallest part of water that can still be considered water.

multicellular Consisting of multiple cells.

mycorrhizal fungi A type of fungi that forms a symbiotic relationship with plant roots, passing nutrients and water to the plant from the soil.

nerves A bundle of fibres that carry electrical messages throughout the body to and from the brain.

nervous system A complex system in the body, made up of the brain, spinal cord and nerves, that allow us to think and move.

nutrients Substances that living things need to live and grow.

organisms A living thing, such as a plant, animal, fungus or germ.

oxygen A gas found in the air that all animals need to breathe.

parasites A living thing that lives inside or on another living thing (its 'host') and benefits from being there – usually by gaining food or nutrients.

petri dish A small round dish with a cover used to grow microorganisms and to look at things under a microscope.

photosynthesis The process through which green plants, algae and some bacteria use carbon dioxide from the air, water from the ground and energy from the sun to make their own food and oxygen.

predators Animals that hunt other animals for food.

rhizosphere The area of soil around a plant's roots, packed with microorganisms, which help the plant grow.

slide A flat piece of glass used to hold objects under a microscope.

spores A cell produced by fungi, some plants and some bacteria in order to reproduce.

symbiotic relationship A relationship that has evolved between two different organisms, in which they both benefit from living together.

unicellular Consisting of a single cell.

vacuum A space that contains absolutely no matter. Beyond a planet's atmosphere, outer space is almost a complete vaccum.